Collins

Integrated Science

for the **Caribbean**

Gene Samuel

Advisors:

Shameem Narine, Nadine Victor-Ayers,
Ishaq Mohammed, Sheldon Rivas

Workbook 3

updated

Collins

HarperCollins*Publishers* Ltd
The News Building
1 London Bridge Street
London SE1 9GF

HarperCollins Publishers
Macken House, 39/40 Mayor Street Upper,
Dublin 1, D01 C9W8, Ireland

Updated edition 2017

10 9 8 7 6

This book contains FSC™ certified paper and other controlled
sources to ensure responsible forest management.

For more information visit: www.harpercollins.co.uk/green

ISBN 978-0-00-826307-2

Collins® is a registered trademark of HarperCollins*Publishers* Limited

www.collins.co.uk/caribbeanschools

A catalogue record for this book is available from the British Library.

Typeset by QBS Learning
Printed in Great Britain by Ashford Colour Press Ltd.

Author: Gene Samuel
Advisors: Shameem Narine, Nadine Victor-Ayers, Ishaq Mohammed, Sheldon Rivas
Illustrators: QBS Learning
Publisher: Elaine Higgleton
Commissioning Editor: Tom Hardy
Editor: Julianna Dunn
Project Manager: Alissa McWhinnie, QBS Learning
Proofreader: Mitch Fitton
Cover Design: Gordon MacGilp
Production: Rachel Weaver

Contents

1 Urinary system

1 What is excretion? _____

_____

[1]

2 What is the purpose of metabolism in the body?

_____

_____

[1]

3 Name TWO organs of the body responsible for excretion.

i) _____

ii) _____

[2]

4 **a)** Write the name of the parts of the urinary system identified by label lines.

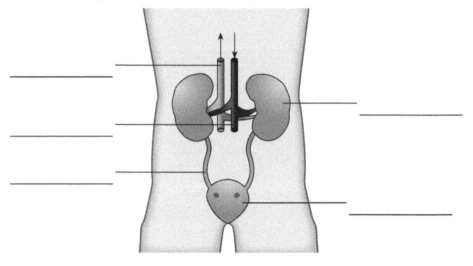

[5]

Say whether each of the following are TRUE or FALSE.

a) The products of metabolism are toxic. _____

b) Blood gets cleaned in the kidneys. _____

c) Only waste products are found in the Bowman's capsule. _____

d) All people with one kidney undergo dialysis. _____

[4]

2 Lungs and skin

1 Excretion in the lungs occurs because of the process taking place throughout the body called:

_____

[1]

2 Name TWO products excreted by the lungs.

i) _____

ii) _____

[2]

3 a) Is it TRUE to say that exhaled air is acidic? _____

[1]

b) Why? _____

_____

[2]

4 On the diagram of the skin, label each part identified by a letter.

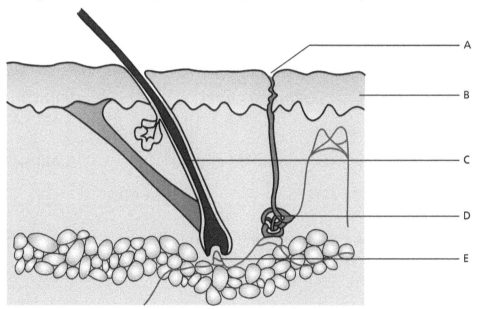

A

B

C

D

E

[5]

5 Name THREE components of sweat.

i) _____

ii) _____

iii) _____

[3]

6 There are TWO important purposes for sweating. They are:

i) _____

ii) _____

[2]

7 Complete the sentences below with the correct words.

Sweat sometimes has an unpleasant odour because of the presence of
_____ in the sweat. _____ is used to lessen the odour
but _____ stops us from sweating.

[3]

3 Water balance

1 From the following list, circle the ways by which the body loses water.

THINKING   DRINKING JUICE   URINATING

DEFECATING   INHALING

EXHALING   HAVING ICE CREAM   DIARRHOEA

SIPPING WATER   SWEATING

[5]

2 On a cold day, a person urinates more frequently than on a hot day. Why is this so?

_____

_____

_____

[2]

3 How does a person become dehydrated?

_____

_____

[1]

1 What does 'reproduction' mean?

_____

_____

[1]

2 Why is reproduction necessary?

_____

_____

[1]

3 **a)** The female reproductive system is shown below.

Name each part identified by a letter.

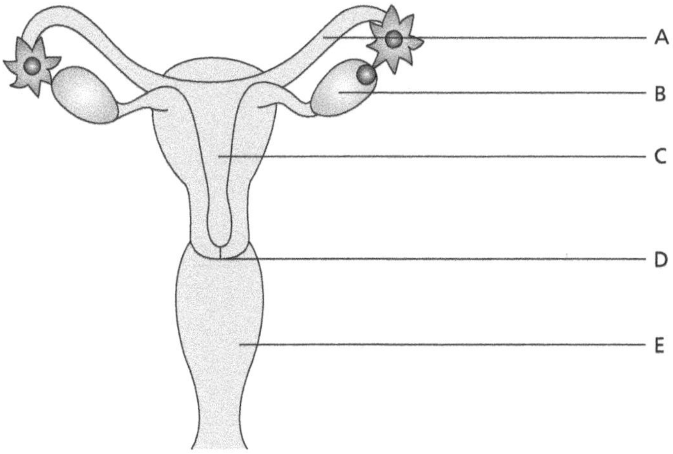

A _____

B _____

C _____

D _____

E _____

[5]

b) State briefly what occurs at each part of the female reproductive system.

A _____

B _____

C _____

D _____

E _____

[5]

For questions 4–6, circle the correct answer.

4 The normal length of the menstrual cycle is:

    a) 21 days   **b)** 28 days   **c)** 40 days   **d)** 31 days.

5 Uterus is another term for:

    a) ovary   **b)** placenta   **c)** womb   **d)** vagina.

6 To nourish the fertilised egg, the uterus builds up:

    a) a blood-rich lining   **b)** fat supplies

    c) water   **d)** a placenta.

[3]

7 **a)** The diagram below shows the human male reproductive system. Name each part identified by a letter.

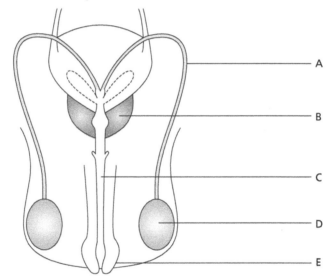

A   _____

B   _____

C   _____

D   _____

E   _____

[5]

b) Each part of the male reproductive system shown in the diagram on page 8 has a specific function.

In the table below, draw lines to match each part with its function.

PART		FUNCTION
A		Produces sperm
B		Contracts to let semen out of the body
C		Passage through which semen leaves the body
D		Duct through which sperm travels
E		Provides the nutrient fluid for the sperm

[5]

For questions 8–12, circle the correct answer.

8 What is the male sex organ that produces and stores sperm?

a) Prostate   **b)** Scrotum   **c)** Testicle   **d)** Vas deferens

9 What is the male cell that unites with the ovum for reproduction?

a) Semen   **b)** Sperm   **c)** Testosterone   **d)** Progesterone

10 Which fluid contains millions of male sex cells?

a) Urine   **b)** Amnion   **c)** Epididymis   **d)** Semen

11 What is the sac holding the testes called?

a) Scrotum   **b)** Vas deferens   **c)** Vesicles   **d)** Epididymis

12 The correct order of the path of a sperm is:

a) vas deferens – epididymis – urethra

b) urethra – vas deferens – epididymis

c) urethra – epididymis – vas deferens

d) epididymis – vas deferens – urethra.

[5]

13 Say whether each of the following is TRUE or FALSE.

a) Both semen and urine can exit through the urethra at the same time.   _____

b) The prostate gland provides the nutrient fluid for the sperm.   _____

c) The testes must always be kept warmer than body temperature.   _____

d) Sperm are made in the vas deferens. _____

e) Oestrogen is the main male hormone. _____

f) Female sex cells are produced in the ovaries. _____

g) The foetus develops in the uterus. _____

h) Several eggs may be produced each month. _____

i) Fertilisation usually occurs in the fallopian tubes. _____

j) Human sperm are made of a head, a body and a tail. _____

k) Male contraception involves cutting and tying the epididymis. _____

l) The uterus is the size of a cherry. _____

[12]

14 Use the clues below to complete the crossword puzzle.

Across

1. Mixture of sperm and other glandular fluids
3. An ovum travels along there
5. A fertilised ovum gets implanted in there
6. When eggs begin to develop in a girl
9. When a woman stops having periods
10. An ovum is released during
12. The male sex cell
14. Shedding of the lining of the uterus

Down

1. Testicle holder
2. Two almond shaped glands producing ova
4. Opening of the uterus
7. Tightly coiled tube found in the testes which stores sperm
8. Tubes connecting ovary and womb
10. The plural of ovum
11. Shape of the opening of the fallopian tubes
13. This contains tissues that get filled with blood to become erect

[8]

3 Communicable diseases of the reproductive system

1 What is meant by the term 'communicable disease'?

_____

_____

[1]

2 Name FOUR communicable diseases.

i) _____

ii) _____

iii) _____

iv) _____

[4]

3 What is meant by the phrase 'symptoms of a disease'?

_____

_____

[1]

4 Give TWO ways by which STDs can be transmitted.

i) _____

ii) _____

[2]

For questions 5–15, circle the correct answer.

5 Gonorrhoea is treated with:

  a) antibiotics   **b)** antiviral drugs

  c) lots of rest   **d)** being very active.

6 To lower a risk of contracting an STD:

  a) use one condom   **b)** use two condoms

  c) bathe before sex   **d)** bathe soon after sex.

7 The most common STD is:

   a) herpes   **b)** HPV

   c) gonorrhoea   **d)** chlamydia.

8 Which of these is a symptom of genital herpes?

   a) Headaches   **b)** Painful blisters

   c) Skin discoloration   **d)** Diarrhoea

9 Which STD is most present in cervical cancers?

   a) HIV   **b)** HPV   **c)** AIDS   **d)** Herpes

10 Which STD causes small, painless, reddish-brown sores on the mouth or on the sex organs?

   a) Syphilis   **b)** Gonorrhoea   **c)** Herpes   **d)** Genital warts

11 If a person shows no symptoms of an STD, it means that he or she:

   a) has no STD   **b)** cannot transmit the STD

   c) can transmit the STD   **d)** is already in the third stage of an STD.

12 What is the difference between HIV and AIDS?

   a) HIV is caused by a virus and AIDS is a bacterial infection

   b) HIV is a virus that causes the disease condition AIDS

   c) There is no difference between them

   d) Scientists have not found the difference

13 Is there a known cure for AIDS?

   a) Yes   **b)** Yes, but it is too expensive

   c) No   **d)** It is by prescription only

14 A person with HIV becomes sick because:

 a) the weight loss is too rapid

 b) the body weakens too quickly

 c) the immune system fails

 d) the body temperature drops a few degrees.

15 How do mosquitoes influence the transmission of HIV and AIDS?

 a) They have no influence

 b) They can transmit AIDS but not HIV

 c) They can transmit HIV but not AIDS

 d) They transmit both HIV and AIDS   [11]

16 Say whether each of the following is TRUE or FALSE.

 a) In STDs, it can take as many as 10 years before
   a symptom appears.   _____

 b) It is possible to get herpes by sharing a glass.   _____

 c) It is easy to tell if your partner is carrying an STD.   _____

 d) Gonorrhoea and syphilis are both bacterial diseases.   _____

 e) There is a medicinal cure for every STD.   _____

 f) You may contract herpes from sitting on a toilet seat.   _____

 g) A negative test result tells you that you do not have an STD.   _____

 h) Both gay and straight men can get an STD.   _____

 i) The contraceptive pill helps to protect against STDs.   _____

 j) Before the 16th century, STDs did not exist.   _____

 k) Teens can get tested and treated without their
   parents knowing.   _____

 l) Diaphragms and cervical caps prevent sperm from reaching
   the uterus. They are also good protections against STDs.   _____

                                                                              [12]

17 Some situations are written in the box below.

Cross out the situations in which it is NOT possible to be infected by HIV.

kissing　　　　　breastfeeding　　　　　touching

unprotected sex　　　　　sitting beside

hugging　　　　　insect bites　　　　　sharing needles

blood transfusion　　　　　cleaning a wound

[5]

4 Environmental impact of human activities

1 Environmental change

1 Give THREE factors that bring about positive environmental changes.

i) _____

ii) _____

iii)_____

[3]

2 An increasing population can bring about environmental changes.

Identify THREE negative changes.

i) _____

ii) _____

iii)_____

[3]

3 Give TWO differences between a rural and an urban environment.

	RURAL	URBAN
i)		
ii)		

[2]

4 Briefly explain how the development of industry influences each of the following.

a) Natural resources _____

_____

_____

b) Acid rain _____

_____

_____

c) Garbage disposal _____

_____

_____

[6]

For questions 5–7, circle the correct answer.

5 Which of these best defines the term 'urbanisation'?

a) A large population emigrating to another country

b) A proportional increase in the population of rural areas

c) A proportional increase in the population of urban areas

d) A large population migrating from the city to the countryside

6 Traffic congestion can contribute to all of the following except for one. Which one?

a) Respiratory illnesses   **b)** Litter

c) Ignoring zebra crossings   **d)** Noise pollution

7 All of the following are affected by urbanisation except for one. Which one?

a) Population growth   **b)** Restricted parking for cars

c) Limited dwelling space   **d)** Increased pollution

[3]

8 Examine the graph below and answer the questions that follow.
The bars show the urban and rural populations and the numbers
of cars and bikes in three counties.

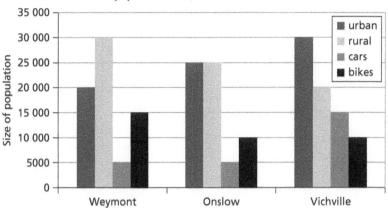

Urban and rural populations and numbers of cars and bikes in three counties

a) What is the total human population of each county?

Weymont _____

Onslow _____

Vichville _____

[3]

b) In which county is:

i) the greatest urban population?

_____

ii) the proportion of urban population to the number of cars the lowest?

_____

iii) the ratio of rural population to bikes 2 : 1? _____

iv) the ratio of urban population to rural population 2 : 3?

_____

v) the lowest ratio of bikes for the rural population?

_____

[5]

c) How does the human population of Onslow compare with the other counties?

_____

_____

[1]

d) Which county might have the greatest air pollution? Why?

_____

_____

[2]

e) If you were asked to choose a county to live in, which would you choose? Explain why.

_____

_____

[2]

9 a) How are plants genetically modified?

_____

_____

[2]

b) Give TWO advantages of genetic modification.

   i) _____

   ii) _____

[2]

c) Give TWO disadvantages of genetic modification.

   i) _____

   ii) _____

[2]

10 a) Give ONE way in which an alien species might be introduced to another place.

_____

[1]

b) Explain why it is possible for the alien species to become a problem.

_____

[2]

11 What is a nature reserve?

_____

_____

[2]

For questions 12–18, circle the correct answer.

12 All of the following are found in vehicle exhausts except for one. Which one?

a) Lead   **b)** Carbon monoxide   **c)** Carbon dioxide   **d)** Hydrogen

13 The largest biotech company in the world also responsible for GMOs in food is:

a) Nestle   **b)** Cadbury   **c)** Monsanto   **d)** Kellogg.

14 What advantage is there in riding a bicycle instead of a motorbike to school?

a) You get exercise   **b)** There is no pollution

c) You get rained on   **d)** A motorbike is quicker

15 All of the following health issues can be caused by air pollution except:

a) coughing   **b)** bowel infections   **c)** bronchitis   **d)** asthma.

16 Clearing trees in catchment areas poses issues to:

a) soil structure   **b)** soil texture   **c)** soil acidification   **d)** soil salinity.

17 GMO stands for:

a) general money order   **b)** genetically modified organism

c) great marketing options   **d)** generically modified organism.

18 Car-pooling has a positive effect on the environment. What is car-pooling?

a) Polishing cars to reduce air resistance friction

b) Washing many cars at a carwash

c) Having many people ride in one car

d) Pulling or towing a broken-down car

[7]

19 Say whether each of the following is TRUE or FALSE.

a) Tree growing raises the level of carbon dioxide in the air. _____

b) On a global scale, the decline in forest areas is due mostly to human activity. _____

c) The world population increases at a rate of 8900 per day. _____

d) The impact of human activity on the environment began over the last 20 years. _____

e) The population of Port-of-Spain is about 60 000. _____

f) Population increases make it easier for an environment to repair itself naturally. _____

g) Urbanisation causes an increase in the population of a town. _____

h) An oil spillage can damage birds that eat fish. _____

i) Pesticides help farmers obtain more food crops. _____

j) As the demands on fishing increase, the fish population also increases. _____

k) The insecticides in food crops have no effect on consumers. _____

l) GM can involve artificially inserting genes into the DNA of animals, not just plants. _____

[12]

2 Habitat protection

1 What is 'deforestation'?

_____

_____

[1]

2 Define 'biodiversity'.

_____

_____

[1]

3 What effect does deforestation have on biodiversity?

_____

_____

[1]

4 **a)** Unscramble the words below to find the countries with the top ten highest deforestation rates.

1 RIBLAZ _____

2 DENAINOIS _____

3 DUNSA _____

4 MIZABA _____

5 COXIME _____

6 Democratic Republic of
   NOCOG _____

7 RAMMANY _____

8 IREAING _____

9 WABBIMEZ _____

10 GAINTAREN _____

[10]

b) On the map below, find each country in **a)** and write its number in the correct place.

[10]

5 Say whether each of the following is TRUE or FALSE.

a) Australia has the largest rainforests.   _____

b) Methane is a greenhouse gas.   _____

c) Indigenous land owners have no benefits from land clearance.   _____

d) Only 50% of the world's species live in the forest.   _____

e) 'Slash and burn' is an irresponsible way to clear land.   _____

f) Species in safe biodiversity zones do not become extinct.   _____

g) Only organic matter contributes to water pollution.   _____

h) Biodiversity refers to the variety of species.   _____

i) Urbanisation impacts negatively on biodiversity.   _____

j) Based on current trends, the world's forests may disappear
in 500 years.   _____

[10]

For questions 6–13, circle the correct answer.

6 Deforestation happens when people try to provide more:

a) water   b) waste   c) timber   d) oxygen.

7 'Slash and burn' releases _____ into the atmosphere.

a) nitrogen   b) hydrogen   c) carbon monoxide   d) ozone

8 Which of the following does NOT directly affect biodiversity?

a) Erosion   b) Weather balloons   c) Predators   d) Rain

9 Pesticides and acid rain both contribute directly to _____ pollution.

a) air   b) noise   c) water   d) soil

10 Which of the following is a poor method of waste management?

a) Incinerating waste   b) Recycling waste

c) Utilising compost sites   d) Using landfill

11 The most common way of getting rid of pests and weeds uses:

a) sewage   b) insecticides

c) pesticides   d) fertilisers.

12 Deforestation worsens the effects of global warming because:

a) the trees would have used up the carbon dioxide

b) there are no trees

c) the trees would have added oxygen to the air

d) trees provide shade.

13 Burning plants contributes to global warming because:

a) carbon dioxide is released during combustion

b) there are no trees to provide shade

c) much oxygen is used up during combustion

d) the sun beats on the bare soil.

[8]

3 Species protection in Trinidad

1 The photos below show some of the protected species of vertebrate in Trinidad and Tobago. Identify each photo with the name of the animal from the following list:

a) Spiny rat   **b)** Robber frog

c) Scarlet ibis   **d)** Luminous lizard

e) Cetaceans   **f)** Howler monkey

g) Leatherback turtle

_____

_____

_____

_____

_____

_____

_____

[7]

2 **a)** Which is the largest nature reserve park in Trinidad and Tobago?

_____

[1]

b) Name TWO endangered species that are protected there.

i) _____

ii) _____

[2]

3 Name TWO major wetland vegetation types that grow in the Nariva Swamp.

i) _____

ii) _____

[2]

4 Give TWO human activities that threaten Trinidad and Tobago species with extinction.

i) _____

ii) _____

[2]

5 **a)** What is meant by the phrase 'an endangered species'?

_____

_____

[1]

b) Choose ONE endangered species in Trinidad and Tobago.
State the method of protection selected by the authorities
to avoid its extinction.

_____

_____

_____

[2]

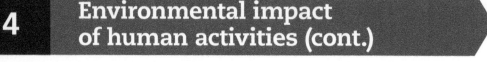

For questions 6–12, circle the correct answer.

6 Which endangered animal often gets caught in boat propellers?

a) Dolphin

b) Manatee

c) Red snapper

d) Porpoise

7 Animals that sleep during the day and roam at night time are:

a) hunters

b) shy

c) predators

d) nocturnal.

8 What should you always carry with you when exploring trails, whether or not you plan to hunt?

a) A decoy

b) Arrows

c) A hunting licence

d) A carcass bag

9 All of the following contribute to animal extinction except one. Which one?

a) Air and water pollution

b) Hunting and fishing

c) The water cycle

d) Larger predators

10 A vulnerable species is one that is:

a) not in danger of extinction

b) never going to be extinct

c) already extinct

d) facing reduced population numbers.

11 All of these severe problems except for one face all species. Which one?

a) Habitat destruction

b) Enhanced reproductive fertility

c) Arrival of alien species

d) Indiscriminate hunting

12 In Trinidad and Tobago some animals are referred to as vermin. These can be killed or destroyed at any time. Which set includes vermin only?

a) Coral snakes, manicou, green parrots

b) Coral snakes, capuchin monkeys, rats

c) Bats, squirrels, brocket deer

d) Mongoose, Fer de Lance, wild hog

[7]

13 Say whether each of the following is TRUE or FALSE.

a) There are over 100 species of snakes in Main Ridge
Forest Reserve.   _____

b) The threat to pawi extinction in Trinidad is from hunting and
loss of habitat.   _____

c) According to the last census, there are fewer than
100 capuchins in Trinidad.   _____

d) The pawi can be found in small numbers in other
Caribbean islands.   _____

e) The ocellated gecko is found in Man Ridge Forest
Reserve only.   _____

f) Aripo Savannas is located in the northern central area
of Trinidad.   _____

g) The habitats of the capuchin are being destroyed
continuously.   _____

h) Only protected vertebrates are present in Aripo.   _____

i) The ocelot is the species of wild cat in Trinidad.   _____

j) The capuchin monkeys live in the swamps.   _____

k) No bird species dwell in swampy lands.   _____

l) The West Indian Manatee is a carnivore.   _____

[12]

14 The common and biological names of some species of insect prevalent in Trinidad and Tobago are given below. Find some pictures of them and stick them in.

a) Ant – *Pheidole aripoensis*	**b)** Katydid – *Cocconotus unicolor*
c) Longhorned Beetle – *Piruapsis antennatus*	**d)** Stonefly – *Anacroneuria isleta*

4 Global environmental changes

1 What is meant by 'global warming'?

_____

_____

[1]

2 Identify TWO situations that may occur because of global climate changes.

i) _____

_____

ii) _____

_____

[2]

3 Explain one negative effect that climate change has on the amount of rainfall.

_____

_____

[1]

4 Give TWO relationships between greenhouse gases and heat radiation that negatively affect the globe.

i) _____

_____

ii) _____

_____

[2]

5 A great amount of heat is trapped in the Earth's atmosphere.
What causes this heat to be trapped?

_____

_____

[1]

6 According to research, the carbon dioxide level on Earth has risen slightly. Examine the diagram below and answer the following questions.

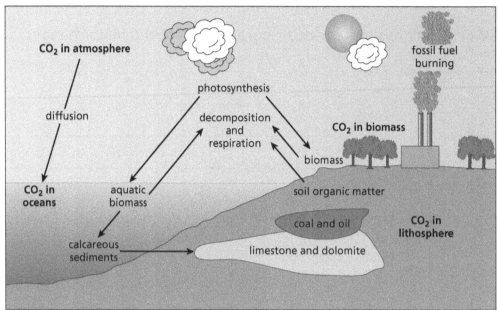

a) Identify FOUR ways in which carbon dioxide enters the atmosphere.

i) _____   ii) _____

iii) _____   iv) _____

[2]

b) Name TWO contributions made by soil organic matter to the environment.

i) _____

ii) _____

[2]

c) What happens to the pH of the ocean seawater as carbon dioxide dissolves into it?

_____

_____

[1]

d) What process reduces the level of carbon dioxide in the atmosphere?

_____

_____

[1]

7 Say whether each of the following is TRUE or FALSE.

a) Greenhouse gases allow energy from the Earth to escape
   into space.   _____

b) Global warming is caused only by human interference
   in the environment.   _____

c) Greenhouses are made of glass; they allow light in but
   trap carbon dioxide.   _____

d) The atmosphere contains poisonous gases from
   human interference.   _____

e) Without the human race, the greenhouse effect
   would not exist.   _____

f) Currently, Brazil has the highest annual rate of deforestation.   _____

g) Climate change refers only to high temperature increases.   _____

h) Since the last century, the sea level has risen by 20.7 inches.   _____

i) Global warming problems can be solved simply by reducing
   the volume of carbon dioxide in the atmosphere.   _____

j) Whereas climate is the average condition over a period
   of time, weather is the current condition for a given place.   _____

k) Without the greenhouse effect, temperatures on Earth
   would be too cold for survival.   _____

l) Smog can cause death.   _____

[12]

For questions 8–16, circle the correct answer.

8 Because of the greenhouse effect:

a) heat is kept away from low-lying areas

b) more light energy is trapped by plants

c) more radiation reflects out of the atmosphere

d) heat is unable to escape from the Earth.

9 With the increase in global warming, storms that hit coastlines will become more intense. These storms are called:

a) tornadoes

b) hurricanes

c) earthquakes

d) tsunamis.

10 The effects of global warming can lead to:

a) deforestation

b) climate change

c) new species

d) an ice age.

11 How long does it take carbon dioxide to leave the atmosphere?

a) 1 year

b) 10 years

c) 50 years

d) 100 years

12 The change in fruit-bearing times of plants is the result of:

a) ozone decrease

b) loss of habitat

c) alien species

d) climate change.

13 All of these steps could help to improve the climate except one. Which one?

a) Stop using chemicals that trap heat on the Earth

b) Reduce the population

c) Use less hot water

d) Prevent earthquakes

14 All of the following are affected by global warming except for one. Which one?

   a) Sea levels   **b)** Coastal flooding

   c) Glacier melting   **d)** Volcanic activity

15 The two gases that make 99% of Earth's atmosphere are:

   a) carbon dioxide and oxygen   **b)** nitrogen and methane

   c) carbon dioxide and nitrogen   **d)** nitrogen and oxygen.

16 The warmth of the atmosphere results from:

   a) air molecules keeping the heat they gain from radiation

   b) plants absorbing carbon dioxide

   c) the mining of fossil fuels such as coal

   d) oxygen absorption by living things.

                                                                     [9]

5   Fighting environmental change

1 List THREE unpleasant characteristics or qualities of waste.

   i) _____

   ii) _____

   iii)_____

                                                                      [3]

2 Give TWO ways in which waste can be combatted.

   i) _____

   _____

   ii) _____

   _____

                                                                      [2]

3 What are biodegradable materials?

   _____

                                                                      [1]

4 Plastics are not biodegradable. However, they have advantages as well as disadvantages.

a) Give TWO advantages of plastic.

i) _____

_____

ii) _____

_____

[2]

b) Give TWO disadvantages of plastic.

i) _____

_____

ii) _____

_____

[2]

5 Give ONE way in which each of the following can help to reduce waste in the areas identified in brackets.

a) Supermarkets (groceries)

_____ [1]

b) Restaurants (dishes)

_____ [1]

c) Banks (statements)

_____ [1]

d) Soda companies (bottles)

_____ [1]

6 This question is about Anna and her meals one Friday.

For morning snack, Anna carried a banana wrapped in aluminium foil and a small-sized bottle of water. For lunch, she had a sandwich wrapped in wax paper, an egg in a sandwich bag and a 250 ml carton of orange juice. For her afternoon snack, there were peanuts in a plastic bag and another small bottle of water. For cleaning up after each meal, she used about six paper napkins. After each meal, Anna threw everything she had used into the classroom bin.

Identify SIX changes that Anna should make so as to reduce waste.

i) _____

_____

ii) _____

_____

iii) _____

_____

iv) _____

_____

v) _____

_____

vi) _____

_____

[6]

For questions 7–13, circle the correct answer.

7 All of the following can be recycled except one. Which one?

a) Milk cartons   **b)** Glass containers

c) Bathroom tissue   **d)** Teeth

8 How many times can glass be recycled?

a) Unlimited times   **b)** 0 times

c) 20 times   **d)** 100 times

9 The average aluminium can is made with _____% recycled aluminium.

a) 0   **b)** 20   **c)** 50   **d)** 100

10 How long does it take an aluminium can to decompose?

a) 5–10 years   **b)** 20–40 years

c) 40–60 years   **d)** 200–500 years

11 When you use rechargeable batteries, you are helping the environment by:

a) recycling   **b)** reusing   **c)** reducing   **d)** recurring.

12 Which of these types of plastic is most dangerous to the environment?

a) PVC   **b)** HDPE   **c)** PS   **d)** PET

13 The label indicating that a material can be recycled is:

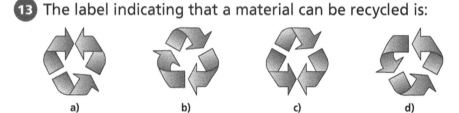

a)   b)   c)   d)

[7]

14 This is the front of an abandoned house in your neighbourhood. You and your friends in an environmental club were asked to transform this neighbourhood eyesore. Below the picture, draw a sketch or a picture of what you think would be best for the neighbourhood.

[5]

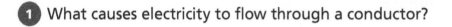

1 What causes electricity to flow through a conductor?

_____

[1]

For questions 2–5, circle the correct answer.

2 The study of stationary electrical charges is called:

a) electrostatics   **b)** electrodynamics

c) electromagnetics   **d)** electrometrics.

3 Which of the sets below contains only conductors?

a) Gold, silver, plastic   **b)** Rubber, plastic, iron

c) Iron, silver, carbon   **d)** Carbon, iron, plastic

4 Electric plugs are made of plastic because:

a) plastic is stronger than many materials

b) plastic is flexible

c) plastic can protect people from electric shock

d) plastic can form various shapes.

5 Insulators do not allow electricity to flow through them. Why are they necessary in circuits?

a) They make circuits safe to handle

b) Electric current will flow only through those insulators

c) Appliances will not work if they are exposed to air

d) Circuits can get very hot

[4]

6 The pictures below show some hazardous situations.

Explain the safety measure needed in each of them.

	HAZARD	SAFETY MEASURE NEEDED
a)		
b)		
c)		
d)		
e)		
f)		
g)		
h)		

[8]

7 Examine the following circuits.

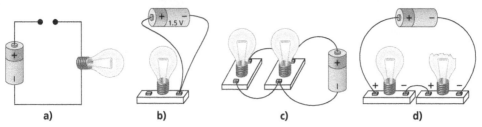

| a) | b) | c) | d) |

Which one(s) show a complete closed circuit?

_____

[2]

8 Use three different coloured markers to trace the path of electricity for each bulb, then indicate below the one(s) that follow a complete circuit.

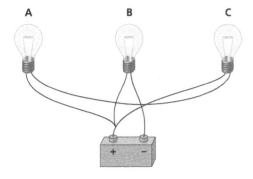

Say YES or NO to indicate whether or not the bulb lights.

A _____

B _____

C _____

[3]

9 Write the names of the following electrical symbols.

	SYMBOL	NAME
a)		
b)		
c)	A	
d)		
e)		
f)		

[6]

10 **a)** In the space below, draw an open circuit diagram using electrical symbols, with an ammeter, one bulb, a switch and a battery of three cells.

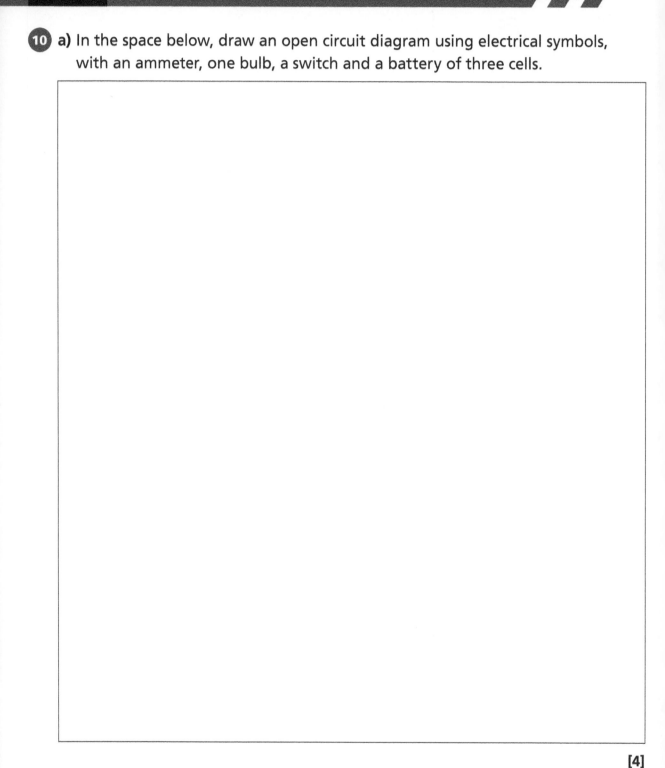

[4]

b) On your diagram, identify the positive and negative terminals of the battery and whether the bulb is lit.

[2]

11 Two circuit diagrams are shown below.

Each cell is rated 1.5 V and all four bulbs are identical.

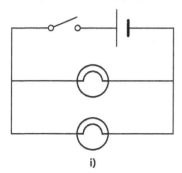
i)

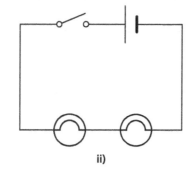
ii)

Use the diagrams to answer the following questions.

a) What type of circuit does each diagram show?

i) _____

ii) _____

[2]

b) When each circuit is closed, in which one will the bulbs be brighter?

_____

[1]

c) If you want all four bulbs to show the same brightness, what adjustment would you make?

_____

_____

[1]

d) If in each circuit one bulb burns out, what happens to the other bulb?

i) _____

ii) _____

[2]

12 Use the diagram below to say whether the following statements are TRUE or FALSE.

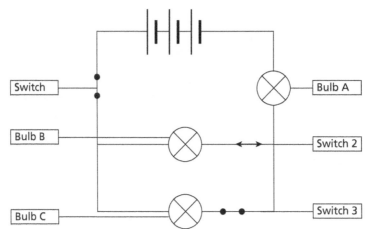

a) Bulb A and Bulb C follow a series circuit. _____

b) If the circuit is open at Switch 1 only, Bulb B will light. _____

c) Bulb B and Bulb C share the voltage. _____

d) Bulb B and Bulb C have a parallel arrangement. _____

e) The arrangement in Bulb B and Bulb C is useful in strings of decorative lights.

_____

f) Bulb B and Bulb C share the current. _____

g) If Bulb B is damaged, Bulb C will not light. _____

h) Switch 3 controls both Bulb A and Bulb C. _____

i) If Bulb A is damaged, both Bulb B and Bulb C will light. _____

j) If only Switch 3 is open, Bulb A will light. _____

[10]

13 Use the clues below to help find the words in this wordsearch.

```
P   T   L   U   C   I   F   F   I   D
G   S   R   Z   N   X   E   X   N   S
S   K   E   C   E   A   L   L   E   D
E   T   P   H   G   M   E   E   K   E
I   N   P   E   A   M   C   N   O   S
R   E   O   M   T   E   T   E   R   L
E   R   C   I   I   T   R   R   B   L
S   R   G   C   V   E   O   G   P   E
K   U   E   A   E   R   N   Y   S   C
J   C   Y   L   F   U   S   E   S   E
```

a) A _____ circuit has only one path for electricity to flow.

b) Electricity is caused by a flow of _____.

c) An _____ is used to measure the current in a circuit.

d) A battery is made up of a number of dry _____.

e) The _____ in a simple series circuit is the same throughout the circuit.

f) In a battery, _____ energy is converted to electrical energy.

g) Electricity is a source of _____.

h) _____ are designed to protect electrical appliances.

i) When an appliance burns out the circuit is _____.

j) Electricity is caused by a flow of _____ charges.

k) The more bulbs that are added to a series circuit, the more _____ it is for current to flow.

l) _____ wires are used to connect appliances.

[12]

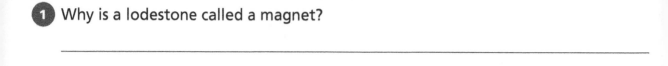

6   Magnetism

1 Why is a lodestone called a magnet?

_____

_____

                                                                     [1]

For questions 2–6, circle the correct answer.

2 Magnet X can hold two steel nails while Magnet Y can hold four. All six nails are identical.

Which is the stronger magnet?

a) Magnet X   **b)** Magnet Y

c) They are equally strong   **d)** More information is needed

3 Which of these pairs of metals are both attracted by a magnet?

a) Iron and steel   **b)** Gold and silver

c) Copper and lead   **d)** Aluminium and zinc

4 A magnet that never loses its magnetism is:

a) lifelong   **b)** energising

c) permanent   **d)** temporary.

5 When magnets repel each other, they:

a) lose their magnetism

b) move towards each other

c) move away from each other

d) swing around.

6 How will these two magnets react when they are brought closer to each other?

a) Attract each other   **b)** Repel each other

c) No reaction   **d)** Swing around

                                                                     [5]

7 The diagram below shows the magnetic field of a single magnet.

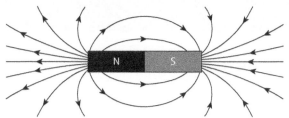

Draw the magnetic fields for the following pairs of magnets.

a)

b)

8 Use the clues below to help find the words in this wordsearch.

```
E  A  T  T  R  A  C  T  O  U
L  C  O  M  P  A  S  S  I  I
D  K  C  T  N  E  K  A  E  W
E  H  T  U  O  S  I  R  O  N
E  L  O  D  E  S  T  O  N  E
N  V  M  B  S  E  L  O  P  Y
U  E  M  A  G  N  E  T  I  C
L  E  P  E  R  D  L  E  I  F
T  N  E  N  A  M  R  E  P  I
K  C  J  N  O  R  T  H  E  Z
```

a) The poles of a bar magnet are _____ and _____.

b) When iron filings are attracted by a magnet they form a _____ _____ pattern.

c) The force of a magnet is strongest at the _____.

d) Like poles _____ each other and unlike poles _____ each other.

e) Big distances _____ the effect of a magnet.

f) A naturally occurring magnet is a _____.

g) Magnets will pick up objects made of _____.

h) A magnetised needle that rotates to show direction is called a _____.

i) A compass _____ always points north.

j) _____ magnets never lose their power.

[13]

9 This diagram shows Oersted's experiment with a compass and part of an electrical circuit.

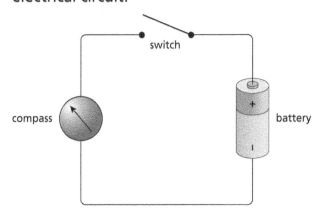

When the circuit is closed, what will happen to the compass needle?

_____

_____

[1]

10 What is an electromagnet?

_____

_____

[1]

For questions 11–16, circle the correct answer.

11 As the current in the wire increases, the strength of the magnetic field:

a) increases   b) remains unchanged

c) stops the field   d) decreases.

12 A relay is used to:

a) ring an electric bell   b) spin a fan

c) start a car ignition   d) heat an iron.

13 The feature that makes an electromagnet useful in a scrapyard is that:

a) it can be turned off and on

b) it cannot be turned off and on

c) it is weaker than a permanent magnet

d) it is stronger than a permanent magnet.

14 The difference between a magnet and an electromagnet is that:

   a) permanent magnets are weaker

   b) electromagnets can be turned off

   c) permanent magnets can be turned off

   d) electromagnets are weaker.

15 When a small current is used in a relay:

   a) it attracts a magnet   **b)** it repels a magnet

   c) it switches off a current   **d)** it turns on a bigger current.

16 Any magnet has two ends. Each one is called a magnetic _____ .

   a) field   **b)** pole   **c)** core   **d)** rod

                                                                                      [6]

17 Say whether each of the following is TRUE or FALSE.

   a) The wire around the core of an electromagnetic should be covered to keep it warm. _____

   b) An electromagnetic field exists only when there is electricity. _____

   c) Every magnet has a north-seeking pole and a south-seeking pole. _____

   d) A solenoid is the soft iron core of an electromagnet. _____

   e) The area around a magnet that behaves like a magnet is a magnetic field. _____

   f) When a magnet is broken, some bits become north and the others become south. _____

   g) A door bell is an example of an electromagnet. _____

   h) The further apart two magnets are from each other, the stronger are the forces that attract or repel them. _____

                                                                                     [8]

7 Light

1 Light

1 Light travels in straight lines called rays. In the space below, draw a ray of light.

[1]

2 A bundle of rays may travel as beams in three different arrangements as shown below. Identify each bundle.

	BEAM	TYPE
a)	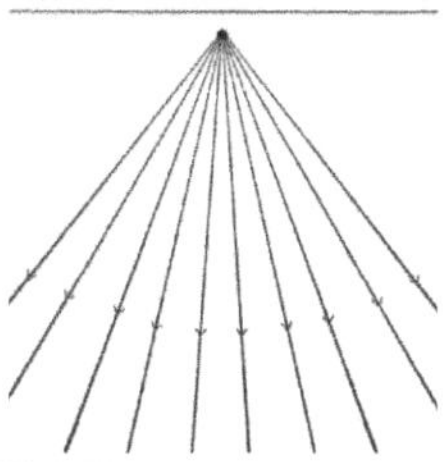	
b)	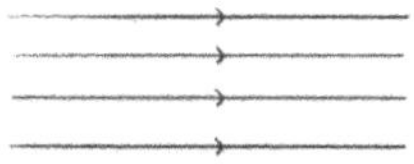	
c)	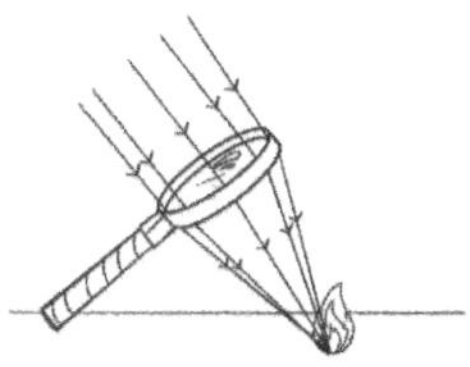	

[3]

3 What type of materials are:

a) luminous? _____

_____

[1]

b) non-luminous? _____

_____

[1]

4 Indicate whether each object below is luminous or non-luminous.

a)

_____

b)

_____

c)

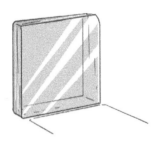

_____

d)

_____

e)

_____

f)

_____

[6]

5 Each of the objects in question 4 emits either hot light or cold light. Write the letter of each object in the correct category below.

i) hot light _____

ii) cold light _____ **[2]**

6 In the table below, give the state of each object and say whether it is transparent (TP), translucent (TL) or opaque (O).

	OBJECT	STATE	TP / TL / O
a)	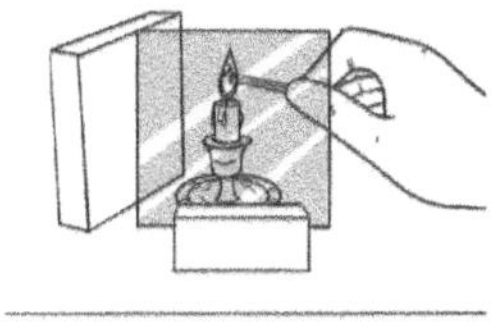		
b)			
c)			
d)			
e)			
f)			

[6]

7 What happens to light rays when they fall on the following types of objects?

a) Transparent objects

_____

_____

b) Translucent objects

_____

_____

c) Opaque objects

_____

_____

[3]

8 The diagram shows an activity involving a cylinder and a lamb.
Various features of the activity have been labelled with a letter.
Write the name of each feature identified by a letter.

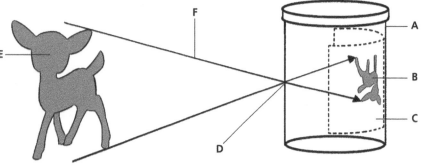

A _____

B _____

C _____

D _____

E _____

F _____

[6]

9 Give TWO properties of the image formed on the screen of a pinhole camera.

i) _____

ii) _____

[2]

10 The size of the object affects the size of the image in the pinhole camera. Draw two diagrams to compare the size of image formed when the size of the object changes.

[6]

11 Examine each diagram below.
Write down the factor that affects the size of the image.

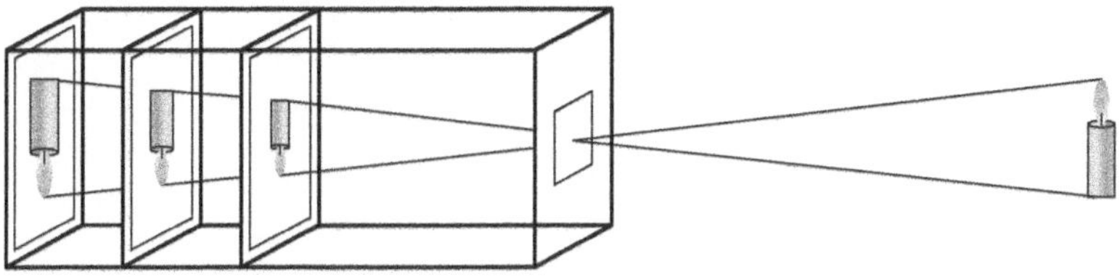

a) _____

_____

[1]

b) _____

_____

[1]

12 What is a shadow?

_____

_____

[1]

13 What type of material forms shadows?

_____

[1]

14 **a)** Complete the diagram below to show the shadow formed by the ball.

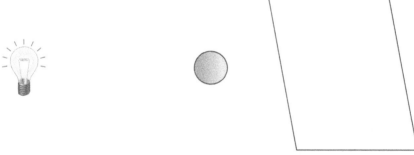

[3]

b) Label all the parts of your shadow diagram. [3]

15 Say whether each of the following is TRUE or FALSE.

a) Shadows are shortest when the Sun is rising. _____

b) As an object gets closer to a light source, its shadow
gets smaller. _____

c) Materials that scatter light are translucent. _____

d) Transparent materials allow light to pass through easily. _____

e) When the Sun is in front of you, your shadow is behind you. _____

f) Planets are good light sources. _____

g) Shadows from a point source are small. _____

h) A penumbra is made when the light source is smaller
than the object. _____

[8]

2 Eclipses

1 What is meant by the term 'eclipse'?

_____

_____

_____

[1]

2 The diagram below shows a solar eclipse.
Write the name of each part indicated by a letter.

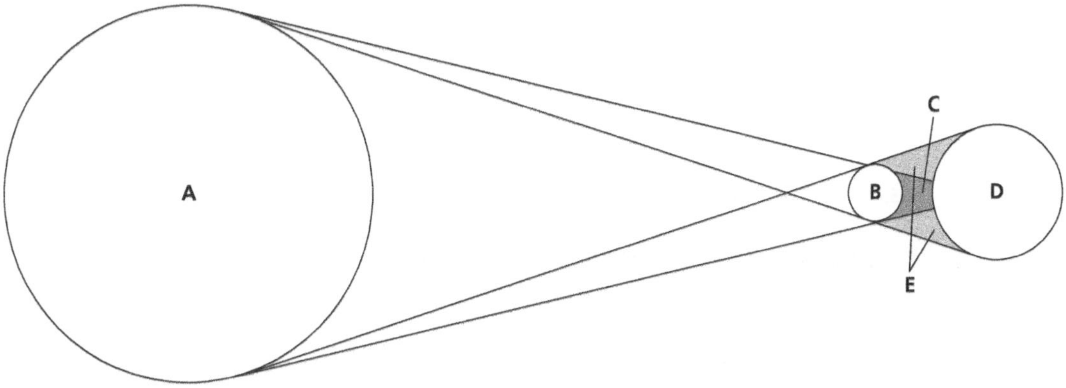

not to scale

A _____

B _____

C _____

D _____

E _____

[6]

3 Look at the diagram below. What would people at positions W, X, Y and Z experience during a solar eclipse?

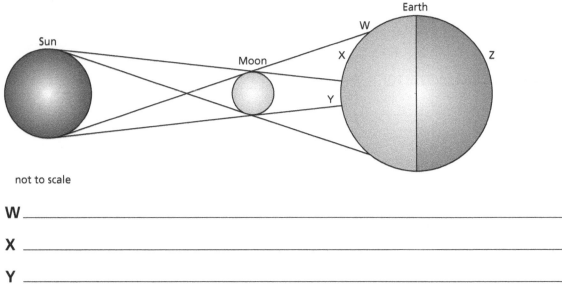

not to scale

W _____

X _____

Y _____

Z _____

[4]

4 Say whether each of the following is TRUE or FALSE.

a) The special sunglasses worn during solar eclipses are solar filters. _____

b) The best view of a solar eclipse is made with binoculars. _____

c) During a solar eclipse, the Moon covers the Sun. _____

d) On rare occasions, solar eclipses occur at night. _____

e) Solar eclipses occur more often than lunar eclipses. _____

f) Solar eclipses occur when Earth passes into the Sun's shadow. _____

[6]

5 The diagram below shows a lunar eclipse.
Write the name of each part indicated by a letter.

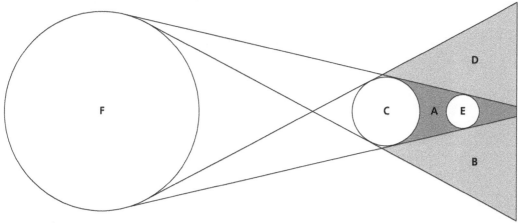

not to scale

A _____

B _____

C _____

D _____

E _____

F _____

[6]

6 Say whether each of the following is TRUE or FALSE.

a) One Moon cycle is about 28 days. _____

b) Only one side of the Moon is seen from Earth. _____

c) When a lunar eclipse occurs, the Earth goes into
the Moon's shadow. _____

d) Lunar eclipses cannot occur during the day. _____

e) A lunar eclipse can occur at any phase of the Moon. _____

f) The Moon looks red because of dust in the Moon's
atmosphere. _____

[6]

7 Look at the diagram below. What would people at positions Q and R experience during a lunar eclipse?

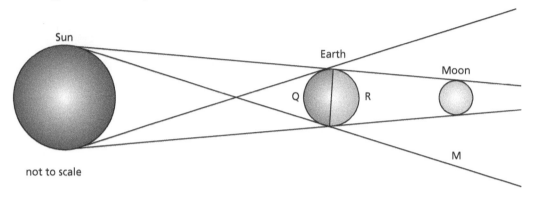

not to scale

Q _____

R _____

[2]

8 **a)** When the Moon moves to location M, people in which position (Q or R) will see it?

_____

b) What will the people at the position in part **a)** see?

_____

[2]

9 Say whether each of the following occurs during a solar or a lunar eclipse.

	SITUATION	SOLAR/LUNAR ECLIPSE
a)	Sun seems to disappear	
b)	Occurs at night	
c)	Special lenses are needed to view	
d)	Moon creates a shadow	
e)	Moon between Earth and Sun	

[5]

3 Reflection and refraction

1 What happens to light when it strikes a smooth surface like a mirror?

_____

_____

[1]

2 The diagram below shows part of an incident ray of light striking a mirror at an angle.

incident ray

mirror

Use a ruler and protractor to complete the diagram as follows.

a) Complete the incident ray.

b) Draw and label:

   i) the normal

   ii) the reflected ray.

c) Label all necessary angles. Add arrows to the rays.

[5]

3 The reflection of an object in a mirror is called its _____.   **[1]**

4 The diagram below shows a trapezium and a triangle. X and Y are the surfaces of two mirrors.

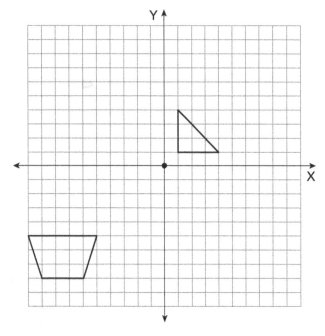

a) Draw the reflection of:

   i)   the trapezium in mirror X

   ii)   the triangle in mirror Y.   **[2]**

b) Name TWO properties that a shape and its reflection have in common.

   i)   _____

   ii)   _____

         [2]

c) What ONE difference is there between a shape and its reflection?

_____

         [2]

5 What is refraction?

_____

_____

[1]

6 Use 'towards' or 'away from' to complete the following sentence:
As a ray enters a more optically dense medium it bends _____
the normal.

[1]

7 In the diagram below, the arrowed lines represent a ray of light.
Study the diagram and give the name of each part labelled by a letter.

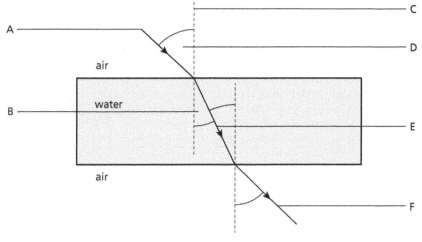

A _____

B _____

C _____

D _____

E _____

F _____

[6]

8 At how many degrees does the normal meet the medium? _____

[1]

9 When someone is short-sighted, where do the light rays that come into their eyes focus to form an image?

_____ [1]

10 The lenses below are used to affect light rays as they enter the eye. Say which type of lens each is.

a)   b)

a) _____ [1]

b) _____ [1]

11 The diagrams below are side views of the human eye.

a) Draw light rays to show the effect of long-sightedness.

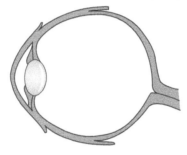

[2]

b) Draw a lens that corrects long-sightedness and show how it changes the light rays.

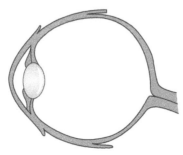

[3]

12 In the diagram below, a fishing bird observes a fish from the side of a lake.

a) Of the two fish shown in the lake, identify which is the object and which is the image.

i) A is the _____

ii) B is the _____

[2]

b) Would it be easy for the bird to obtain its meal? Explain why or why not.

_____

_____

[2]

13 The refractive index of an optical medium is calculated as:

$$\text{refractive index} = \frac{\text{real depth}}{\text{apparent depth}}$$

Calculate the refractive index of water in a pool if a coin 6 m deep appears to be at a depth of 4.5 m.

[2]

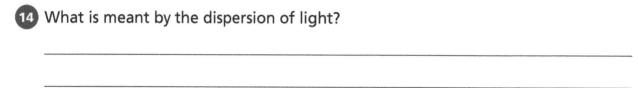

14 What is meant by the dispersion of light?

_____

_____

[1]

15 A small beam of white light passes through a prism in a dark room. Show what happens to the ray of light as it enters the prism and also as it leaves the prism.

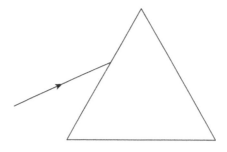

[3]

16 Two prisms are arranged as shown below. A small beam of light is allowed to pass through the two prisms, as indicated. Show what happens to the ray of light as it enters the prisms and leaves them.

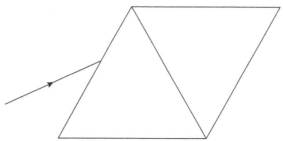

[2]

17 How are rainbows formed?

_____

_____

[1]

18 To cause a rainbow, what does each water droplet act like?

_____

_____

[1]

19 The colours of the rainbow are:

YELLOW   BLUE   RED   GREEN   VIOLET   ORANGE   INDIGO

Using these colours, draw a rainbow in the space below.
Use coloured crayons if available; if not, use a pencil and label the colours in the order that they occur.

[3]

20 Say whether each of the following is TRUE or FALSE.

a) The colour of an object is seen because of colour transmission. _____

b) Images are seen in a mirror because of reflection. _____

c) Light bends as its speed changes. _____

d) A solid transparent object that can separate light
   is called a pyramid. _____

e) Translucent materials provide both privacy and light. _____

f) Light is an invisible form of matter. _____

g) A real image can never be formed on a screen. _____

h) Concave lenses produce larger images. _____

i) Light travels through all liquids at the same rate. _____

j) The image in a plane mirror is always upright. _____

k) When light travels from plastic to air, it speeds up. _____

l) You cannot see clearly through frosted glass because light
   is absorbed. _____

[12]

8   Chemical bonding

1   The basics

1 How many groups of elements are there in the periodic table? Consider just the first 20 elements.

_____

[1]

2 Which group(s) contain the most non-reactive elements?

_____

[1]

For questions 3–11, circle the correct answer.

3 Which elements are good heat conductors and have high boiling and melting points?

a) Metals   b) Non-metals

c) Poisonous   d) Solids

4 Ionic bonds occur between non-metals and _____.

a) solutions   b) metalloids

c) non-metals   d) metals

5 All elements in Group 8 are:

a) highly reactive   b) monatomic

c) metallic   d) very dense.

6 Most metals can bond with all of these except for one. Which one?

a) A gas   b) A non-metal

c) Another metal   d) Chlorine

7 Which of the following pairs of elements can form an ionic bond?

a) H, Ar   b) Na, H

c) H, Ne   d) He, Ne

8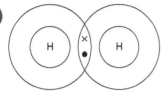

The above combination of atoms shows:

a) an ionic bond   **b)** a covalent bond

c) two ions   **d)** a helium molecule.

9 Which pair of elements is most likely to form a bond?

a) He, N   **b)** Ne, Na

c) H, N   **d)** F, Cl

10 Diatomic molecules contain:

a) two different molecules

b) two identical atoms

c) two diatoms

d) two ions.

11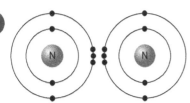

When the two atoms shown above bond:

a) they will each share three electrons

b) they will each lose three electrons

c) the second one will lose its outer electrons

d) the first one will lose its outer electrons.

[9]

12 Choose the correct description in the right-hand column to match the diagram in the left-hand column.

DIAGRAM		DESCRIPTION
a)		one molecule of oxygen gas or ionic bonding of two oxygen atoms
b)		ionic bonding of a chlorine molecule or one chlorine gas molecule
c)		two atoms of neon or one molecule of neon
d)		will form an ionic bond or will form a covalent bond
e)		complete bonding or incomplete bonding
f)		ionic bonding of NH_3 or covalent bonding of NH_3
g)		a hydrogen and carbon bond or an incomplete combination

[7]

13 Give the charge of each of the following.

a) Neutron _____

b) Proton _____

c) Electron _____

[3]

14 What is an ion?

_____

_____

_____

[1]

15 Say what causes an ion to be:

a) positive

_____

_____

_____

[1]

b) negative,

_____

_____

_____

[1]

16 Fill in the information for each of the atoms given below.

	ATOM	NUMBER OF ELECTRONS TO BE GAINED OR LOST	IONIC CHARGE
a)	F	_____ electrons to be _____	
b)	Li	_____ electrons to be _____	
c)	Cl	_____ electrons to be _____	
d)	K	_____ electrons to be _____	
e)	Al	_____ electrons to be _____	
f)	O	_____ electrons to be _____	
g)	Mg	_____ electrons to be _____	

[7]

17 For each pair of atoms, give the charge each atom will have when electron transfer or ionisation occurs.

a)

_____   _____   [2]

b)

 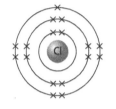

_____   _____   [2]

c)

_____   _____   [2]

d)

 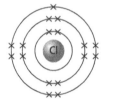

_____   _____   [2]

e)

_____   _____   [2]

18 Say whether each of the following is TRUE or FALSE.

a) Group 2 elements bond well with Group 8 elements. _____

b) Hydrogen and chlorine can form both ionic and
covalent bonds. _____

c) Metals do not bond with all gases. _____

d) When metals bond with non-metals, metals gain electrons. _____

e) Covalent bonds occur when diatomic gases form. _____

f) In covalent bonding, electrons are gained. _____

g) When an atom loses or gains electrons, it becomes an ion. _____

[7]

19 Complete the sentences by filling in the blanks.

a) When atoms _____ electrons, they become negative ions.

b) One atom of Mg combines with one atom of O to form a/an

_____ bond.

c) An atom that loses or gains electrons becomes a/an _____.

d) Metals lose electrons so they become _____ ions.

e) When a Cl atom gains an electron, it gets a charge of _____.

f) Polyatomic molecules are made up of _____ atoms.

g) During bonding, when electrons cannot be gained or lost,

they are _____.

h) The combination of atoms formed in a covalent bond is
called a _____.

i) Electrovalent also means _____.

j) Nitrogen, N, has 5 valence electrons. Each nitrogen atom shares

_____ when a diatomic molecule is formed.

[10]

2   Chemical reactions

1 Substance A reacted chemically with substance B to form substance C.

  a) Describe TWO observations that may be made during the reaction.

    i) _____

    _____

    ii) _____

    _____

         [2]

  b) Give TWO differences that may exist between substance C and the two individual substances that formed it.

    i) _____

    _____

    ii) _____

    _____

         [2]

2 Give ONE physical property of each reactant and product.

  a) hydrogen   +   oxygen   →   water

    _____   +   _____   →   _____

         [3]

  b) carbon   +   oxygen   →   carbon dioxide

    _____   +   _____   →   _____

         [3]

  c) sodium   +   chlorine   →   sodium chloride

    _____   +   _____   →   _____

         [3]

For questions 3–15, circle the correct answer.

3 When a chemical reaction occurs, it always produces:

a) reactants

b) a change of state

c) different substances

d) a precipitate.

4 A + B combine chemically to form C + D. The reactants are:

a) A and B

b) C and D

c) A, B, C and D

d) AB + CD

5 A substance which speeds up a chemical change but does not react with the components of the reaction is a _____.

a) precipitate

b) catalyst

c) product

d) reactant

6 A chemical equation shows how substances _____.

a) vaporise

b) react

c) bond

d) inflate

7 A _____ added to an acid forms a gas that gives a squeaky pop.

a) metal

b) metal oxide

c) metal carbonate

d) metal hydroxide

8 Atoms _____ during chemical reactions.

a) make new bonds

b) are created

c) are destroyed

d) get lost

9 A change of _____ always accompanies a chemical reaction.

a) energy

b) nuclei

c) order of elements

d) state

10 The reaction of acid with _____ always produces a gas.

a) an alkali

b) a metal oxide

c) a carbonate

d) a hydroxide

11 The arrow in an equation means that:

   a) the two sides are equal

   b) the products flow into reactants

   c) a reaction is happening

   d) electrons are exchanged.

12 $2Mg + O_2 \rightarrow 2MgO$ indicates that:

   a) 2 atoms Mg react with 2 atoms of O

   b) 1 atom of Mg produces one atom of O

   c) the equation has the same number of atoms on either side

   d) magnesium must react with two molecules of oxygen.

13 An example of a chemical change is:

   a) dissolved gas evolving from boiling water

   b) melting brass to make a door knob

   c) dissolving a vitamin C tablet in cold water

   d) the sublimation of dry ice.

14 Which of the following is a chemical equation?

a) lemonade (liquid) + carbon dioxide (gas) → soda (liquid)

b) water (solid) + heat → water (liquid)

c) carbon (solid) + oxygen (gas) → carbon dioxide (gas)

d) sea water → salt (solid) + water (liquid)

15 An example of a reversible change is:

a) magnesium brightly burning

b) calcium carbonate fizzing with acid

c) white zinc oxide changing yellow with heat then white on cooling

d) soap cutting grease.

[13]

16 On the periodic table below, write:

a) the group numbers

b) the symbol of atoms

c) the valence of the atoms that become ions.

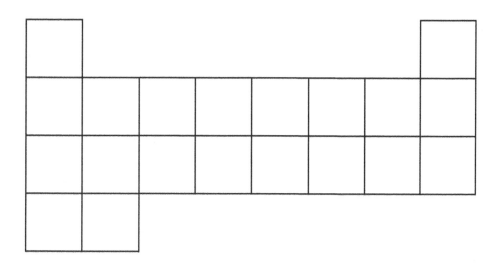

[5]

17 Say whether the statements following are TRUE or FALSE.

a) The strength of a bond affects the physical properties of substances.

_____

b) The substances made from covalent bonding are poor electrical conductors.

_____

c) Substances formed from ionic bonding have low melting and boiling points.

_____

d) In ionic bonding, the compound becomes magnetic. _____

[4]

18 Each illustration below represents a chemical equation.
Underneath each illustration, write the equation using formulae.

a)

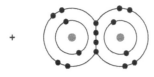

_____

[1]

b)

H_2 Cl_2

_____

[1]

c)

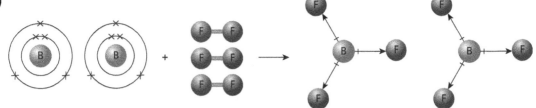

_____

[1]

1   Acids and alkalis: the basics

1 What is an indicator?

_____

_____

_____

[1]

2 Name TWO indicators.

i) _____

ii) _____

[2]

3 Write down the pH range for:

a) acids _____

b) alkalis _____

[2]

4 What is the difference between an acid with pH 2 and one with pH 6?

_____

_____

_____

[1]

5 Name TWO everyday items that are acidic.

i) _____

ii) _____

[2]

6 Is saliva acidic? Explain why.

_____

_____

_____

[1]

7 Give TWO everyday items that are alkaline.

i) _____

ii) _____

[2]

8 Carbon dioxide is expelled from the body all day. Is it acidic or alkaline?

_____

_____

_____

[1]

9 If an alkali is spilt onto the skin, how does it feel?

_____

_____

_____

[1]

10 Say whether each of the following is TRUE or FALSE.

a) All substances are categorised as either acidic or alkaline. _____

b) Acids can be either strong or weak. _____

c) Alkalis change red litmus paper to blue. _____

d) Some weak acids are called hydroxides. _____

e) Formic acid is found in ant venom. _____

f) Ammonia is acidic. _____

g) One property of acids includes being corrosive. _____

h) Alkali means dry. _____

i) Acetic acid gives vinegar a sour taste and strong smell. _____

j) Neutral solutions have a pH of 0. _____

k) Alkalis are soluble bases. _____

[12]

11 The information below relates to acids and alkalis.

A is an acid   B is a base   C is neutral

D is the set of alkalis   E is a salt   F is sour

G is neither acidic nor alkaline   H is an indicator   I has pH 3

J resulted from an A + B reaction   K resulted from A + H   L is bitter

Correctly place the letter for each item of information in the following Venn diagram.

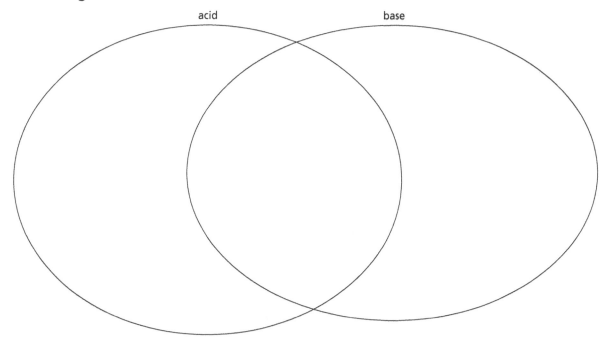

[12]

For questions 12–22, circle the correct answer.

12 Vinegar, fruit juices and sodas are categorised as:

a) strong acids   **b)** strong bases

c) weak acids   **d)** weak bases.

13 Solution A has a pH of 4. Which of the following would neutralise it?

a) Some sodium carbonate   **b)** Some vinegar

c) Purified water   **d)** Distilled water

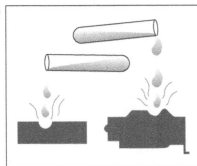

On which of these acids would you see the symbol above?

a) Citric   **b)** Hydrochloric

c) Ascorbic   **d)** Carbonic

15 Which of these is true of all bases?

a) They are alkalis   **b)** They are soluble

c) They are colourless   **d)** They neutralise acids

16 Farmers use lime to neutralise their acidic soil. Lime is:

a) a base   **b)** a very weak acid

c) a sour fruit   **d)** used as it rots.

17 Which statement is FALSE? Acids and alkalis neutralise each other to form:

a) salt and water   **b)** a new neutral product

c) a neutral product   **d)** water and gas only.

18 All acids change _____ litmus paper to _____.

a) red, blue   **b)** blue, red

c) yellow, red   **d)** pink, blue

19 Universal indicator is green and can indicate both acids and alkalis. It is therefore:

a) neutral   **b)** slightly acidic

c) slightly alkaline   **d)** a base.

20 Of the solutions below, which has a pH of 12?

    a) Dilute hydrochloric acid   **b)** Ammonia

    c) Dilute sodium hydroxide   **d)** Sea water

21 Vinegar is acidic and bleach is alkaline. Which statement is FALSE?

    a) Red litmus changes to blue with bleach

    b) Red litmus remains red in vinegar

    c) Blue litmus changes to red with bleach

    d) Blue litmus changes to red in vinegar

22 Which statement is TRUE about acids and bases?

    a) Not all acids neutralise all bases

    b) All acids neutralise all bases

    c) Bases become stronger when acids are added to them

    d) Acids become stronger when bases are added to them

[11]

23 Give the chemical formula for these common acids used in the laboratory.

    a) Hydrochloric acid

_____

    b) Sulphuric acid

_____

    c) Nitric acid

_____

[3]

24 The neutralisation of an acid and an alkali produces a salt and water. Give the name of the salt formed from the acids and alkalis given below.

    a) sodium hydroxide + nitric acid

_____

    b) calcium hydroxide + hydrochloric acid

_____

c) magnesium hydroxide + sulphuric acid

_____

d) lead hydroxide + nitric acid

_____

e) zinc hydroxide + hydrochloric acid

_____

f) copper hydroxide + nitric acid

_____

[6]

25 Complete the sentences with the type of salt made from each acid.

a) The salt made from hydrochloric acid is a

_____

b) The salt made from sulphuric acid is a

_____

c) The salt made from nitric acid is a

_____

[3]

26 The names of the salts from neutralisation are given below. Complete the table by identifying the hydroxide and the acid from which each one was formed.

	SALT	HYDROXIDE	ACID
a)	calcium nitrate		
b)	copper chloride		
c)	zinc sulphate		
d)	potassium chloride		
e)	aluminium nitrate		
f)	lead sulphate		

[6]

27 Write the products of the following neutralisations.

a) iron hydroxide + nitric acid

_____

b) zinc hydroxide + hydrochloric acid

_____

c) ammonium hydroxide + sulphuric acid

_____

d) calcium hydroxide + nitric acid

_____

e) lead hydroxide + hydrochloric acid

_____

f) potassium hydroxide + nitric acid

_____

[6]

2   Acid–base reactions

1 Some substances are called metal oxides. How are metal oxides formed?

_____

_____

_____

[1]

2 When an oxide and an acid react, what are the products of their neutralisation?

_____

[2]

3 Give the name of the salt formed from the given acids and oxides.

a) magnesium oxide + nitric acid

_____

b) sodium oxide + hydrochloric acid

_____

c) lead oxide + sulphuric acid

_____

d) iron oxide + nitric acid

_____

e) copper oxide + hydrochloric acid

_____

f) potassium oxide + nitric acid

_____

[6]

4 Write the products of the following reactions.

a) ammonium oxide + nitric acid

_____

b) zinc oxide + sulphuric acid

_____

c) calcium oxide + sulphuric acid

_____

d) lead oxide + nitric acid

_____

e) magnesium oxide + hydrochloric acid

_____

f) calcium oxide + nitric acid

_____

[6]

5 When carbonates or hydrogen carbonates are neutralised by acids, fizzing occurs. What does the fizzing indicate?

_____

_____

[1]

6 What should be done to confirm which gas bubbles out of the reaction of a carbonate and an acid?

_____

_____

_____

[2]

7 Write the products formed from the given acids and carbonates.

a) magnesium carbonate + nitric acid

_____

b) potassium carbonate + hydrochloric acid

_____

c) copper carbonate + sulphuric acid

_____

d) sodium carbonate + nitric acid

_____

e) zinc carbonate + hydrochloric acid

_____

f) lead carbonate + nitric acid

_____

[6]

8 When acids react with metals, what gas is given off?

_____

_____

[1]

9 How do you test for the presence of the gas evolved by the reaction of a metal and an acid?

_____

_____

_____

[2]

10 Write the products of the following reactions.

a) magnesium + hydrochloric acid

_____

b) potassium + nitric acid

_____

c) sodium + sulphuric acid

_____

d) zinc + nitric acid

_____

e) iron + hydrochloric acid

_____

f) calcium + nitric acid

_____

[6]

11 Sodium chloride can be made using hydrochloric acid in different reactions. Write the FOUR chemical reactions that produce sodium chloride.

i) _____

ii) _____

iii) _____

iv) _____

[8]

For questions 12–17, circle the correct answer.

12 In the chemical equation

aluminium hydroxide + hydrochloric acid → X + aluminium chloride

X represents:

a) aluminium oxide   **b)** water

c) hydrogen   **d)** oxygen.

13 Which of the following elements does NOT naturally form a diatomic molecule?

a) Hydrogen   **b)** Boron

c) Oxygen   **d)** Nitrogen

14 A metal combines with oxygen to form:

a) water   **b)** metal oxide

c) diatomic molecule   **d)** covalent compound.

15 An acid and metal react to form:

a) halogen and salt   **b)** hydrogen and water

c) salt and hydrogen   **d)** halogen and hydrogen.

16 A chemical reaction always:

a) requires oxygen   **b)** uses one reactant only

c) forms new products   **d)** involves elements.

17 The elements in calcium carbonate are:

    a) calcium and carbon

    b) calcium and oxygen

    c) calcium, carbon and oxygen

    d) calcium, water and carbon dioxide.

         [6]

18 Say whether each of the following is TRUE or FALSE.

    a) When an acid reacts with a hydroxide, oxygen gas evolves.   _____

    b) A metal oxide reacts with an acid to produce salt and
        water only.   _____

    c) An acid reacts with a metal and hydrogen gas evolves.   _____

    d) In neutralisation, acids and alkalis react to form salts.   _____

    e) Oxides such as calcium oxide form hydroxides with water.   _____

         [5]

19 An acid reacts with a substance and fizzing occurs.
Explain what you would do to test the gas, and the results you would get,
if the gas were:

    a) carbon dioxide

    _____

    _____

    _____

    _____

         [2]

    b) hydrogen.

    _____

    _____

    _____

    _____

         [2]